BR

Sheila Buck

ARTHUR H. STOCKWELL LTD.
Elms Court   Ilfracombe   Devon
Established 1898

© Sheila Buck, 1999
First published in Great Britain, 1999
All rights reserved.
No part of this publication may be reproduced
or transmitted in any form or by any means,
electronic or mechanical, including photocopy,
recording, or any information storage and
retrieval system, without permission
in writing from the copyright holder.

British Library Cataloguing-in-Publication Data.
A catalogue record for this book is available
from the British Library.

By the same author:
  Africa Remembered (Travelogue)
  From West to East and Beyond (Travelogue)
  It's Never Too Late (Travelogue)
  The Websters (Novel)

ISBN 0 7223 3268-8
Printed in Great Britain by
Arthur H. Stockwell Ltd.
Elms Court Ilfracombe
Devon

Contents

23rd May 1982 — 21st December 1987	5
21st December 1987 — 24th August 1998	19
24th August 1998 — 9th April 1999	27

List of Illustrations

Braddie – five and a half years old	Cover
Braddie as a puppy – six weeks old	7
Braddie, on window seat – one year old *"In comfort"*	10
Braddie, with owner, on a moorland walk – two years old	13
Braddie, with front paws on sill – three years old *"Who is that?"*	16
Braddie, with red football – five years old *"Wait"*	21
Braddie, with a piece of football – five years old *"Please play"*	23
Braddie, on a walk – eight years old *"Go fetch it"*	24
Braddie, with Kong – ten years old *"I am waiting. Come on"*	28

23rd May 1982 — 21st December 1987

After the untimely death, at five-and-a-half years, of our first Border collie, Arthur (my husband) and I decided that we would not have another dog. We were left with poignant memories of her and felt sure that no other dog could replace her. She was such a loyal and companionable friend who brought us much joy.

However, as the days passed we realized that we could not continue life without another. We lived on a moor which was a perfect environment for a dog.

At one-day-old on 23rd May 1982, we chose her from a litter of eight. Her mother was a pedigree springer spaniel and her father a working Border collie. You may wonder why we chose her at such a young age. The farmer, who owned her parents, did not want to keep any of the remaining pups, the reasons for which we did not question. The local vet very kindly assisted us. The choice was not easy, at that age they all looked gorgeous, some more voluble with their shrill squeals as they pushed one another for the best position to reach their mother's teats to gain their share of her milk. There were five males and three bitches. We had decided to have a bitch and so, there only being three, our choice was easier to make. I picked one up and as she lay in the palm of my hand, squealing as loud as she could, the vet said, "She will develop into a good strong dog". And so it was that this little black and white "bundle" of one-day-old came into our lives.

We arranged with the farmer that we would collect her at the end of July. He allowed us to visit her during the time she was with her mother.

What should we call her? We wanted a short name, easy for us to say and for her to answer to when called. Many names came to mind, such as Nell, Beth, Bess, Flash and the like. One day Arthur suggested "Brad" as she was born near the village of Bradworthy. I said that we could not call her Brad as it was a boy's name and so we decided on Braddie.

During the next few weeks, we visited her often and noticed the gradual changes in her growth.

Braddie as a puppy – six weeks old

She spent her early days in a dark corner of a calf pen where she had been born. She seemed a lonely little pup. We presumed that she was missing her brothers and sisters and could only rely on the comfort and care she received from her mother when she appeared. When her mother was with her she did not resent us being there and was content for us to cuddle Braddie, as we now called her. In spite of her smallness and age, she appeared to have a will of her own.

Day by day she grew, her eyes opened and soon she became a round fat puppy. She had black ears, black hair around her eyes which even then were a beautiful brown. We called her Braddie each time we saw her and hoped that she would soon recognize her name and our voices. She loved the farm and spent a lot of her time digging in a sand pit with her mother and we hoped that this fun was not a forerunner to digging up our garden!

At last the time came for us to take her home. She sat on my lap but was obviously not too happy as she kept on whimpering. It was all so strange and frightening for her. We knew that once she had settled she would be happy with her new surroundings.

When we arrived home we took her round to the rear garden of the cottage where she would be free to run around. She had not been there long when we saw her on the moor trotting in the opposite direction to the cottage. She had pushed her way through two small gates which, after collecting her from the moor, we secured with wire netting. One thing she learnt from that was that if she met wire netting she was not allowed beyond it!

We had been given a beer barrel for her to sleep in, which she loved as it was dark and cosy inside and reminded her of her sleeping place at the farm. This was put in the utility room.

That night she seemed to settle quite happily, but at 3 a.m. the next day, Arthur aroused me to say that she was crying. I hurried downstairs and found her very unhappy. Thinking that she wanted to relieve herself, I carried her onto the moor to no avail. Once indoors again, I warmed some milk for her which she would not drink, so I tried some cold which she did. I put her back into her barrel after cuddling her and left. There was not another sound and by the morning she was full of fun and ready for breakfast.

I used to take her several times a day for walks on the moor and gave her obedience lessons. She soon learnt to "stay", "sit", and "wait", etc., thoroughly enjoying herself. At the same time she grew, lost her puppy hair and developed a beautiful shiny coat. Her tail gradually lengthened and she resembled a Border collie rather than a springer spaniel.

Braddie, on window seat – one year old
"In comfort"

She was good at retrieving anything that we threw for her. She would hide until we threw a ball or a ring, then chase after it, pick it up and dash back with it to drop it near where she had been hiding. We could never get her to drop it at our feet. She was full of fun and when in the garden was happy chasing a football and delighted when she managed to burst it.

In the day she had a wooden box in the garage to sleep in, most of which she chewed. We soon learnt that she would come quickly when I whistled her even when she was chasing rabbits on the moor, during which time she would yelp, quite definitely thinking that she would catch them.

We discovered fairly early on that cats for her were meant to be chased. We had never encouraged her but through her entire life she hoped that she would reach the cat but never did. The nearest she could get was if the cat went up a tree or perched on a fence where she would sit, bark furiously and wag her tail.

A more serious problem for us was that she disliked other dogs. She did not go for them but would regard them with scorn and disdain, growling in the deepest voice that she could deliver. This caused us great embarrassment and not entirely friendly looks from the owners of the other dogs. She became more aggressive if she was approached by the enemy. All through an encounter her tail would be wagging and after passing all danger she would give us her doggie grin and an expression in her eyes as much as to say "Didn't I do well".

Storms were another matter and something we always dreaded. Suddenly she would start to tremble and become restless. After about five minutes of this we would hear thunder and see flashes of lightning. In no way could we comfort her, and whilst the storm was in progress, she would go from one room to another, trembling and panting. We noted that through the years whenever she was stressed she would tremble. She was indeed a very sensitive creature, but most intelligent.

She was one of routine and suspicious of any change in the daily run of the house. One day was like another, so that she knew where she was but, if a door which was normally open was suddenly closed, an object removed from its usual place, the noise of some article being wrapped and excited whisperings, she would sit, emit a long sigh, and place her chin against the ground. She would then follow me until she managed to push her nose around the offending door and see the suitcase. Then she would sit on a familiar garment intended for the suitcase, look up at me with her beautiful questioning brown eyes which said, "Are you

*Braddie, with owner, on a moorland walk
– two years old*

going away?" Then a wag of her tail, a tentative bark and off she would trot to contemplate this rather worrying change of routine.

When the time came to take her anywhere in the car, to the vet or for a holiday, she would disappear or sit in one of her favourite spots in the garden with her back to the car and her head half turned, hoping that we had not seen her. Once in the car she settled and was always well behaved and never attempted to leave the boot to join us.

We had her spayed when she was quite young as she had a false pregnancy. Unfortunately, when we arrived at the vets, he was away. His wife suggested that we left her at the surgery. She was put into a fairly dark cage and was there for quite a few hours before the vet arrived. The strange thing was that from then on she would no longer use her barrel for sleeping. We could only think that her time in the vets cage was very stressful.

We loved caravanning, and so did Braddie. Her first trip was to Gloucestershire. We stopped at a lay-by on our way to give her a run. I took her into some fields which had a low grassy bank dividing them. Having let Braddie off the lead, she rushed ahead and suddenly a fox appeared. They both spotted each other simultaneously and were off. Braddie let out a scream of delight as she streaked after the fox as he was running for his life. I was helpless for no amount of whistling would bring her back. They raced across the field and were soon out of sight. I decided that I would never see her again, as I did not know the layout of the land and had visions of her being run over if she came to a road. I returned to the caravan and told Arthur what had happened. He went in one direction to look for her and I followed, as best I could, the route that she had taken. Suddenly I saw her in the distance, nose to the ground as she returned along the track she had taken. Finally she arrived at my feet completely worn out, mouth wide open and her long pink tongue dripping moisture. I picked her up and carried her back the short distance to the caravan. I could not scold her, I was so relieved to have her back and that she had, young as she was, returned to us and bravely used her sense of smell to do so.

Arthur was a keen fly fisherman and we had many enjoyable evenings fishing in the local rivers. Braddie came with us, of course, and used to spend much of her time sitting beside Arthur and watching, like him, for fish to rise and full of excitement if a catch was made.

One of her assets was that she loved people. She always made anyone who came to the cottage welcome and she loved to have people to stay.

Braddie, with front paws on sill – three years old
"Who is that?"

I suppose her walks on the moor were what she enjoyed most. During her very early years, I was painting butterflies found in Devon for a friend. There were plenty on the moor and we had much fun flushing them out of the undergrowth and bushes. She pretended to try to catch them but never did. There were many other attractions — rabbits, exciting scents of cats, other dogs and humans.

She spent most of each day out of doors, policing up and down our driveway and barking at the ponies on the moor if they dared to approach our fence and take a nibble at our trees and shrubs. Much to her annoyance, they ignored her efforts, which made her all the more eager to restrain them. If we were out, we would find her patiently sitting by the gate waiting for our return, her tail wagging furiously when she saw us.

Once in the cottage she would retreat to her favourite spot which was in the middle of the couch with Arthur and myself on either side of her. She had her own rug on the couch and would never attempt to sit anywhere other than in the middle with her head pressed down on my lap. This choice of the couch came about when she had been spayed. She decided that she was a delicate patient and alas needed comfort from us. So for the first few days, I would have her on my lap. Eventually jumping on the couch to lie between

Arthur and myself became a habit which she enjoyed to the full for the rest of her life.

We seldom had to reprimand her. A change in the tone of our voices would be sufficient for her to completely alter in shape and looks. Her head would drop with her ears well back and a sombre expression in her eyes. She appeared to get smaller as her tail disappeared under her body which began to tremble. She did her best not to be seen and would try to hide without success and would wait for any punishment that might come. When she decided that this was not forthcoming she would retreat with dignity and apology until her body would return to its normal shape, her tail reappear and the love she yearned for once more given. Her response was then a nuzzle into one's face or hand and a violent wagging of her tail knowing that she was forgiven.

21st December 1987 — 24th August 1998

It became necessary for us to move from the cottage to a bungalow. We were not particular as to which county we should try. Our main concern was to find one with a reasonably large garden for Braddie and in the country giving access to good walks. She was then in her prime at five years old.

We travelled many miles into Wiltshire, Somerset, Devon and Cornwall, always taking Braddie with us. She knew which bungalows and gardens she approved of and at times would not bother to leave the car to inspect.

Finally we chose a four-bedroomed bungalow with half an acre garden in a rural environment. Unfortunately there was no room for our caravan, so this we had to sell. It was a great disappointment as it had given all three of us so much pleasure.

Braddie soon settled and loved the garden. Her walks over the fields were a delight with plenty of rabbits to chase.

It was not long before she found herself a "boyfriend". She met him with his master during a walk. He was called Ben and was of the same cross breed as herself. He was about the same age but bigger than her. It was love at first sight. They continued to meet almost daily. When she saw him she would let out a loud greeting and rush to him after having paid her respects to his master. When I had to be away, Ben's master would take them both together for a walk.

After Arthur's death in 1994, Braddie missed him and was quite unhappy for a while. She did not like anyone sitting in his usual place on the couch. She would growl and become stressful when anyone tried. However, she eventually accepted that he was no longer with us or part of the family.

Another couple living in the village became her great friends and mine. He came to help me in the garden and mowed the lawns. Braddie liked him at their first meeting. She used to hear him coming, watch him parking his car and trailer whilst standing with her front paws on the fence and serenade him with yelps of delight and barking. Then she would rush round the garden to the gate where he would enter and then besiege him until

*Braddie, with red football – five years old
"Wait"*

she was given the biscuits he had brought for her. Her day was made. She would follow him back and forth and watch him mow. This became a routine and Tuesdays were one of her happiest days.

His wife was also a great friend. Braddie was very spoilt by her. She enjoyed her love, attention and the biscuits *she* gave her. And appreciated the many times that she looked after her when I was away.

All in all her life in the bungalow was a happy one. She grew into a beautiful healthy dog and was a very loyal companion to me. I could not have asked for anything more than the love and trust she gave me. She was always so honest and never complained.

Alas, as we all do, she began to show her age. Grey hairs appeared in her white legs and her muzzle. She was still very lively, always ready for a game which at this time was with a ragger.

She decided after Arthur's death that she would sleep in my bedroom. I moved her bed into my bedroom and for the rest of her life she always slept there. I came to value her company and felt secure that she was there.

The years went by and we both aged. Braddie became deaf, her muzzle even greyer with almost white hairs surrounding her eyes, but even then

*Braddie, with a piece of football – five years old
"Please play"*

Braddie, on a walk – eight years old
"Go fetch it"

she was a lovely looking dog. People could not believe her age which, in 1997, was fifteen. She was still very lively but became more dependent on me. She still enjoyed our trips to Salisbury where we stayed with a friend. Braddie used to spend her time sitting by the patio window in my friend's dining room which looked onto the garden. The attraction was the neighbouring cats who frequented the garden. Braddie would be almost hysterical with barking at them. In most cases she was successful in getting rid of them.

24th August 1998 — 9th April 1999

The time came when I could no longer manage the garden and so I moved to a smaller bungalow not far away, taking Braddie with me.

I was rather apprehensive about the move as far as Braddie was concerned. She was now sixteen years of age and definitely showing her age. She was deaf and her sight was failing. She no longer required long walks but still enjoyed her freedom in the garden. And she was lively.

The bungalow to which we were moving had no garden of its own but the surroundings were such that I could use for exercising her and were attractive. There were ducks on the lake and plenty of squirrels running around. I also had a small conservatory attached to the bungalow.

However, she soon settled and I developed a

Braddie, with Kong – ten years old
"I am waiting. Come on"

routine for her and she was happy. One of her joys was to visit my neighbours and soon she was invited in and I must say spoilt by them all.

After a few weeks, I could leave her indoors whilst I was shopping, etc., which I had never had to do in the past. She was so good and would sit looking through my patio doors waiting for me to return. She seemed to know when I had parked my car and was ready, with her tail wagging, an expectant look in her eye, for my return, and what a joyous greeting I received!

At the end of January 1999, she seemed to fail a bit. On her walks she became slower and found them rather tiring. She spent a lot of time sleeping in her place on the couch and was always glad of my lap on which to lay her head. To gain my attention she would tap one of her front legs on my thigh, nuzzle my hand and give out a long sigh.

Now she is at peace. She carried away with her so many years of my own life. When she just sat loving and knew that she was being loved were the moments precious to her. The look through her beautiful eyes made me think that she knew I was really thinking of her.

She was always so patient if I left her for a few hours. She greeted my return with affection, no complaining but wagging her delightful Border collie tail which told me everything and how pleased she was to see me come home.

There is nothing more precious than the love and trust of a dog who is, as I believe, one's best friend.